My Journey From Wrongfully Accused to Success

Mike Powlas

Webster Falls Media™

Books • Films

www.websterfalls.com

The stories in this book are based on the recollection of the author. Some details, specifics or names may have been
changed or deleted in order to protect the privacy of those involved.

© 2020 by Mike Powlas

All Rights Reserved.
No part of this book may be reproduced in any form, including electronic, digital or mechanical means, without written permission of the authors. Reviewers may quote brief passages in a review only.

Published by Webster Falls Media LLC

www.websterfalls.com

First Edition

ISBN (softcover): 978-0981687261

Printed in the USA

To My Family.

Acknowledgements

There are many people who helped me through life, during my time of being held in jail, and who helped my family keep going during that challenging time in my life.

Johnnie Lewis was there with me on the inside as we went through the Hell of being in jail. He helped keep my spirits as high as they could be at the time. We frequently read the Bible together and listened to the radio at night. We distracted ourselves from what was happening in our life often by following high school football games in the area.

I owe a huge amount of gratitude to Roger Ryan. He not only came to see me often when I was in jail, but he was there when I was finally released after it was proven I was innocent. He also called my wife frequently to add a voice of encouragement and tell her everything would be okay. When I was released, he told everyone he could that if they needed any HVAC work done, I was the guy to call. That helped me get back on my feet as soon as I could.

My sister, Charlotte Barnhill, was a major help to my wife while I was being held in jail. She checked on her on at least a weekly basis and also helped with some everyday tasks.

A lifelong friend, Betty Brannon, was of great encouragement when I was released. She lives hundreds of miles away now, but would frequently speak with me through the digital world to talk about the old days of growing up together. Those conversations helped eased the anxiety and stress of putting a home and business back together.

Neil and Glenn Powlas are my brothers. I am very thankful for their incredible help to my wife while I was being held for so long. They were always just a phone call or a text away if she needed help. They frequently gave her rides to the store when she needed things for the family.

Thank you to Dorothy Rockmere who wrote the most letters to me while I was in jail. Her letters were very encouraging as I waited for the day I could be back with my family.

My mother-in-law, Paula Carper, was a lifesaver in giving her daughter, my wife, a break from the stress of trying to carrying on without my help during those challenging days. She would keep the children for a day or overnight to give my wife some free time to take a break to handle some chores or write me a letter.

Thank you, too, to my wife's brother, Brian Thomas. He helped with food and other things needed by my family for everyday life until I got back home.

Chapter One

On February 1st, 2012, I walked out of the New Hanover County jail in Wilmington, N.C. as a free man. Except for being transported in a van to court hearings, it was the first time I had actually been outside.

The reality was that I was supposed to be released the day before, but the District Attorney's office had failed to get the official release documents to the jail. My attorney and I both thought they did that deliberately in retaliation. You'll see what they were retaliating against later.

The 24 hours I sat and waited seemed longer than the hundreds of days I had been already kept behind bars. It was hard to believe I would soon be a free man. I would be home and trying to reconstruct some kind of life for my wife, me and our children. My wife had been the one to shoulder the worst of the nightmare. It would take some time to get all back to some new kind of normal.

I had been accused of a crime many react to with more emotion than they do a murder charge.

Actually, I was not dwelling on the entire process of being incarcerated for something I did not do. Nor, was I drowning in anger over how my opinion of the legal system had changed by what had happened to me. I was brought up in a family that respected law enforcement and our court system. This experience had changed my entire belief in a system that I was taught usually worked. Instead, I was focused on getting home and back to work so I could provide for my wife and family. Within 48 hours of being released, I was back on the job, rebuilding a company I started.

All of the days I spent behind bars gave me an opportunity to look back and evaluate my entire life up to that point. My memories took me back to my simple childhood, surrounded by a great family, including a mother and father that everyone who knew them respected. I held on to faith I would eventually be back in that community, reunited with my family.

It was a family that now included a wife and children. I wanted them to eventually have fond memories similar to the ones I had growing up. They were reflections I had no idea would one day include jail and a terrible accusation.

Looking back, I was very fortunate to have such great recollections of my youth. Many in jail do not have them. Instead, they look back on a life of broken families, parents on drugs and other memories they would rather forget than remember. Instead, my life seemed more like a family TV show from the 60s, as you will see.

Chapter Two

I grew up in Wilmington, North Carolina. It was in a community known as Seagate situated between Wilmington and Wrightsville Beach. Until very recently, my wife, children and I lived in the same home my parents lived in when they were married.

My mother was born and raised in Southport, located south of Wilmington where the Cape Fear River meets the Atlantic Ocean. Southport is a small, but popular coastal town reached by a few highways and by way of a very popular drive-on ferry that runs between the end of U.S. Highway 421 at Fort Fisher and travels the Cape Fear River to Southport. In the summer months, the ferry runs almost every 45 minutes and is filled with tourists making the 35-minute ride. Taking the ferry saves you from at least a 35-mile drive from Wilmington down to

Southport and is loaded with scenic views along the route.

If Southport sounds familiar, it could be because it has become famous as the location where several popular movies and TV shows were filmed. Nicholas Sparks' *Safe Haven*, *The Secret Life of Bees* and the Stephen King TV series *Under the Dome* are a few productions that used Southport locations. In fact, you can take a golf cart tour of the film locations in Southport during the summer vacation months.

My father grew up in the Seagate community of Wilmington, where I lived until recently. I don't recall my parents ever talking about how they actually met. However, they must have met when they were young since they married in their early 20s.

My mom and dad obviously met after my mother's mom moved from Southport to Wilmington into a home on Wrightsville Avenue, not far from my father's house. It could have been very likely they met at the business my father ran.

My dad owned a Gulf-branded service station back in the days when you actually got service when you filled up. You would pull up to a pump, get the gas pumped for you while the attendant cleaned your windows and checked your oil. All of that service and gas was only about 35 cents a gallon then! I can picture my grandmother pulling into that Gulf station, with my mom in the car, only to have my father be the one to provide the service.

Not only was my father a local, respected businessman, he was also very active in the community. He was a part of the Seagate Volunteer Fire Department and was one of the men who formed the all-volunteer department. He eventually was elected chief.

When the Seagate Volunteer Fire Department first formed, they only had a small piece of land with no building. Their only fire truck sat in the open on that property.

In those days, local volunteers were alerted to a fire call by a siren that would sound loud enough for everyone in the community to hear. The firemen would then make their way quickly to the fire truck so they could respond. My father had the telephone company run a line from his service station to the fire department property so he could activate the siren when a call came in.

I have no direct memories of my father's days at his service station since he had transitioned into a building repair business about the time I was born. However, I do remember him talking frequently about his adventures and experiences at the Gulf station.

My mother was a busy, stay-at-home mom, which was much more common in those days. While she was always volunteering to help with projects in the community and at church, she never held a paying job outside the home.

Most memorable about my mom was her dedication to church. If the doors of Seagate Baptist Church were open, she was there. She did teach Sunday School on occasion, but mostly preferred to remain low-key and attend all the services and events at the church. To this day, just like my mother did, my father attends every service unless he is under the weather.

My grandmother was another very close and memorable member of the family. She is fondly remembered by all of us along with her extended family she had at work. She was the head cook in the

Winter Park Elementary School for almost three decades. She was definitely a fixture in the school and was loved by all the students, their parents and the school staff.

I had great role models at home as a child, but I wasn't the only kid in the house. There were others at home, too.

Chapter Three

When all was said and done, my parents ended up with five children. I was next to the youngest.

The first to make their way into the world of the Powlas' home was my sister, Charlotte. She is now married with three children of her own and lives just north of Wilmington in Rocky Point. Next came two older brothers, Charles and Neil.

Charles lives in Jacksonville, N.C., the home of Marine Corps Base Camp Lejeune. He followed in my father's footsteps and became a member of the Seagate Volunteer Fire Department. Then, he moved on to become a professional firefighter for the City of Jacksonville.

While working as a firefighter, he made extra income in building and building repair. He and my father created the company after my father sold his service station.

After Charles came Neil, and then a younger brother joined the family. His name is Glenn.

With a large family, holidays became big events. You could most likely describe our family holidays as traditional, including the fare on Thanksgiving.

The remaining family still gets together at Thanksgiving and it is usually held at my home. That began when I became the one with the most children. It was easier for everyone to come here than it was for us to gather up our crew and travel. Even extended family, including my mother's sister, who now lives in Georgia, travels here for holiday get-togethers with the family. The entire holiday adventure repeats itself around Christmas time.

Like most of us, I have a lot of memories from my youth centered around school days. To a certain extent, the timing of my school days was fortunate, considering Wilmington's history. Not long before I entered school, the city was still recovering from a long period of racial unrest. In fact, Wilmington was frequently on the national nightly newscasts and made major newspaper headlines. During that period, it was not uncommon for there to be frequent curfews in place and the National Guard was deployed to help the local police. By the time I hit school, those days of unrest had calmed substantially, thank goodness.

I spent my elementary school days, the first grade through the fourth, at Bradley Creek School, very close to Wrightsville Beach. Next came the fifth and sixth grades at another school. During those days, the school was named Tileston. The building remains as a school but under a different name.

There was a very special teacher I was particularly fond of in the fourth grade at Bradley Creek School. Her name was Mrs. Wood. She was, hands down, the most dedicated teacher I ever had or even heard of. Everyone, including students and parents, noticed the way she bent over backwards to help students in her class that were struggling. She was never a teacher who subscribed to the practice of just passing a student through the system. She wanted everybody to succeed.

Mrs. Wood lived within walking distance of my family's house, so we all knew her as a neighbor in addition to being a teacher. I liked her so much I would some days get off the bus in front of my house and walk to hers just to sit and talk. I never saw her show any partiality to students who were those listed as "academically gifted." She treated those who struggled with equal respect.

It is easy to back up how people felt about Mrs. Woods not based on just words and opinions, but by her actions. It was not unusual to see her spending one-on-one time with those who needed help. Years later, I learned she even would take time on teacher workdays, when the schools were closed for students, and tutor her struggling students at the school. In fact, she was also known to have gone to some students' homes after hours to tutor them there. She was an incredible lady and first-class teacher. She was also a big contributing factor to me liking school. I even liked school after I entered the usually-challenging junior high school days.

Chapter Four

I doubt there is a parent alive who didn't brace themselves for the body-and-mind changing years of junior high school, more frequently referred to as "middle school" today. The emotional and physical changes going on during the period someone approaches the teenage time of their life is normally a trying time for all involved. In that respect, I consider myself a lucky guy.

My transition from the elementary school years to junior high went relatively smoothly compared to many others I saw. I chalk that up to the fact I had already created a major goal for myself and had become fascinated with two big subjects – electronics and automobiles. I knew I wanted a career that involved one or both.

The seventh through ninth grade years for me took place at Roland Grice School. Unlike today in most places, at that time you did not go to high school until the tenth grade.

If anything major changed for me in the transition from elementary school to junior high school it had to do with books. I wasn't much of a reader in the early school years, but that changed at Roland Grise School. I began to love to read and learn new things. I was quickly developing a love of cars and knew I wanted to learn everything I could about them. I took that interest into high school where my auto-repair teacher had selves of books on the subject and I read them all. I wanted to learn things faster than he was teaching them.

I wasn't interested in sports when I was in school. However, it was required we have regular physical education classes. On occasion, they would take us to play basketball at a nearby high school, Laney High School. We would play with the high school students. One of the guys we frequently played basketball with was a guy by the name of Michael Jordan. To this day, when I see him on television, I can honestly say, "I played basketball with him." Of course, that was before he became a household name and incredibly wealthy.

Looking back, I now know my interest in learning how things worked was inspiration passed down from my father. He may have sold his service station shortly before I was born, but he continued to work on our family car and other things around the house. There were certainly no leftover parts when he fixed anything, whether it was the car, our lawnmower, or even after removing a room from a house and rebuilding it with substantially better quality than the original construction.

The focus today seems to be on earning a piece of paper with some academic degree on it. My father proved you could definitely be a genius without that. He never graduated high school, but I admired all he could do with the combination of his mind and his hands. He is, hands down, one of the smartest men I have ever known.

I took the fascination I had with fixing and repairing things I witnessed my father doing right on into high school. I attended New Hanover High School in Wilmington. Many famous folks spent time walking through the doors of that high school, including newscaster David Brinkley, Meadowlark Lemon of the Harlem Globetrotters, and the woman who would eventually become Madame Chiang Kai-shek, whose husband was the leader of the Republic of China between 1928 and 1975.

Another fortunate part of the timing of my school days was the fact there was substantially more opportunity for vocational education then. Schools were loaded with all kinds of training, ranging from construction to even placing students in paid apprenticeships in industrial settings. Of course, I immediately signed for up for auto shop training.

The teacher for auto repair at New Hanover was a man named Mr. Devane. I've had the pleasure of crossing paths with him and a coach at New Hanover during those days, Mr. Miller, several times since graduating. The auto shop was a full-sized, well-equipped one at New Hanover.

I would end up with credit for four separate car repair courses by the time I graduated, and they were credits with real experience behind them. With a full-scale shop at our disposal, we went well beyond the book theory of how autos worked, we learned how to completely rebuild a car engine by actually doing it. A fellow classmate, Matt Wall, and I rebuilt a car engine in high school auto shop. He now owns his own car repair business and is no doubt good at it because of the training at New Hanover High School. It's sad students with a gift in working with their hands, as well as their minds, don't have as much access to the vocational training we had in high school.

My interests did fall into the mechanical and electronic areas, but that did not mean I did not focus on the rest of my education. In fact, a few teachers started calling me "Mister Sponge," because they said I soaked up everything I read or learned.

The opportunity with so much variety between the vocational training I was getting in high school and the academic work kept me engaged. As a result, there were some years I had perfect attendance. I'm not sure I would accomplish that in high school today with the death of so many vocational training opportunities.

There was something else I learned while spending all those high school days working on cars. I decided I was not cut out to work in one space for a long period of time. The thought of being glued to one shop for over 40 hours a week didn't sound appealing to me at all. Fortunately, while I still enjoying working on cars, I also had developed an interest in all things electrical. I was fascinated with electronics. So, I studied electricity and electronics with the same passion I did car repair. I knew electricians rarely worked in one location for long periods of time and I liked the thought of that mobility. Between the training I received in auto shop and the study of electricity, I have been able to combine what I've learned in all I studied with work I have done since 1988 – HVAC installation and repair, as well as working with computers.

However, there were some stops along the way before I landed jobs and created my own company.

Chapter Five

While I was studying auto mechanics and electronics, along with the required subjects at New Hanover High School, I primarily focused on school. What spending money I made came primarily from doing mowing and yard work. Unlike many of my fellow classmates, I didn't need much money because I had not seriously entered the dating world.

I certainly noticed the girls in school, but it wasn't the single-minded focus of some of my friends. I didn't even go to the prom in my junior or senior year.

This is not to say I didn't date at all. There was a girl named Betty who went to New Hanover and also to our church. We spent quite a bit of time together, even dating off and on for almost three years. Life pretty much changed things. Betty became very busy at work and her mother passed away. Then, her job took her to

Florida and then to Texas. Eventually, we concluded we weren't meant to be in a romantic relationship, but we became great friends. Thanks to Facebook, we still check in on each other's lives from time-to-time.

I graduated from New Hanover High School in 1984 with more than enough credits. That was because I took more than the required elective courses because they were on subjects that interested me. As I said, I focused mainly on school in those days. Immediately after graduating, I hit the work world. I decided to pay some dues for serious trying to land work in one of the fields I was really interested in.

There is no doubt in my mind that my interest in working hard came by way of my parents. My father was a hard-working man. He would head out for work early in the morning and there were many evenings he did not get home until 7:00 or 8:00 p.m. when my mother would have to reheat some dinner for him. While my mother didn't have an outside-the-home-job, she put her heart into the volunteer work and family responsibilities with the same amount of effort my father put into his work.

Another influence passed down to me by my parents was my lack of interest in parties and drugs. Alcohol, the drug of choice in my high school days, was something my mother was adamantly against. She would even study the ingredients of cough and cold medicines to make sure they did not contain alcohol. Neither my mother or father lectured us often on drugs. Their actions spoke louder than any words.

Today, I may have five wine coolers a year during some special occasions, but that is it.

With a high school diploma in hand, I started looking for work. I decided to stay at home for about three months after graduation and then I found my own place in Castle Hayne, a community just north of Wilmington. I was saving money by living a home and was planning to save money for a car. However, I lucked up in the transportation department when my grandmother decided to give me her car. It was a 1965 Rambler Classic 660 with a 282 single-barrel and it was a straight six. I had transportation and was ready to go to work!

My first official job was at Bojangle's, a fast-food chain that originated in North Carolina, famous for their chicken and biscuits. The restaurant was located on College Road in Wilmington which was a good distance from Castle Hayne.

Just before I landed the job, my luck in getting the Rambler made a U-turn. I started having serious problems with the transmission. Since the transmissions in Ramblers had an aluminum casing, you could not find any shops willing to work on them and give you any kind of warranty or guarantee. My father convinced me to sell the car rather than be hit with an expensive repair bill on a transmission with no guarantees.

Looking back, there have been times I wished I held onto that car even if I had to buy another one to get around. The man I sold the Rambler to eventually found a transmission in a junk yard. He fixed the car and still has it to this day. He enters it into car shows. I found out by accident that he still had the car. In a nostalgic mood, I began looking online for a Rambler 660. I began to discover a lot of them were on the car show circuit and I found out my old car was one of them.

"The only mileage being added to it now is when I drive it up the ramp and onto the trailer to take it to a car show," the guy who bought the car from me said. The car currently has only about 2,000 more miles on it than when I sold it to him around 1985.

Now, stuck without a car and not enough funds to get another one fast, I went to plan B to get to my new job at Bojangle's. I put a ten-speed bicycle to work. Since it was a good ways to work and I was a biscuit maker on the morning shift, I left for work at 4:00 in the morning in order to insure I would get to work on time. That bike was my work transportation for almost a year.

Riding a bike that far to work was challenging. While there was not too much traffic that time of morning to deal with, it was a different story on the ride home. I had to keep my eyes peeled for drivers not paying attention. Plus, the weather could be tough. I had become the Bojangle's equivalent to a postal carrier. "Neither rain, sleet, snow or gloom of night would keep me from making my appointed rounds" as a biscuit maker. Fortunately, snow and sleet are rare in southeastern North Carolina.

There was a 24-hour convenience store along my route to work and it became my regular stop. Ironically, even though I was headed in to make great breakfast biscuits, I bought a premade sausage biscuit every morning at the store to eat before my shift. Those convenience store biscuits didn't come close at all to the biscuits at Bojangle's, but I needed to eat before I made the first batch at work.

Several years ago, I was in a Lowe's Hardware store where my brother Neil worked at the time. One of his fellow workers approached and we both thought we had definitely seen each other before, but we could not place where. After thinking about it for a few days, it finally hit me. The next time I was in Lowe's I approached the guy and said, "Let me have a sausage biscuit." Turns out he was the guy who worked the night shift at the convenience store where I made my early morning stop on the way to work.

My trusty bicycle became much more than transportation to and from work during my days at Bojangle's. It was keeping me in the best shape of my life. In addition to going to work, I often rode it around my neighborhood and even occasionally made the ten-mile trek out to Wrightsville Beach. That was during a time when people paid more attention to their driving and were not distracted staring at their cell phones. I don't think I would be that brave to ride a bike everywhere today.

When I wasn't working, I spend time with friends. One great friend is David McMillan. We shared a love of vehicles and even built a few go-carts together.

David's choice in cars was always Mustangs. He was obsessed with them and eventually bought a model of Mustang in which only 100 of them were ever produced. He still has that car.

David was also a member of the fire department, like my father and brother were. He eventually got married and moved out of town for a long while. We still kept in touch. He returned to the area and went to work for the New Hanover County Sheriff's Department. He would have some things to say when I was placed in jail years later.

My work at Bojangle's continued for a year. I had worked my way up to the head biscuit maker. However, that restless part of me was kicking in, not wanting to be tied down working at one specific location. Plus, I was anxious to find work where I could put my interest in mechanical and electrical skills to work. I would find a job that would let me use both.

Chapter Six

After working for Bojangle's, I landed a job briefly working for an electrician before going to work in the heating and air conditioning business, known in the field as HVAC. I went to work for Butler Electric in Leland, which was across the bridge spanning the Cape Fear River from Wilmington.

"Across the bridge" in those days was a frequently used term to separate Leland and Wilmington. With the Cape Fear River being a separation point between Brunswick County, on the Leland side, and New Hanover County on the Wilmington side, there had been quite a rivalry created between the two areas. Referring to somebody or someplace "across the bridge" had a negative connotation to it. That sounded like sports rivalries to me, which I thought was silly.

Getting that first job in HVAC happened quite by chance. The owner of Cape Fear Heating and Air was a man named Al Batts. When he was a toddler, my grandmother had been his babysitter. His family lived on Wrightsville Avenue, not far from College Road, which was close to my grandmother's home, which is now a doctor's office.

One day, while visiting my grandmother, we began to talk about my work.

"I think I'd like to get into heating and air," I said.

"You don't like electrical work?" she asked.

"I just stay in one place for too long."

"I know someone in that business," she said.

I went to Cape Fear Heating and Air and applied for a job. In less than a week, Al Batts called me to come in. We talked and he hired me. The business was so close, I actually rode a skateboard to work. Here I was, 22 years old, and in a career that would last a long time. It was good timing that I asked for the job when I did. It was May and getting hot in the Wilmington area, so demand for HVAC services was growing fast. Plus, since the completion of I-40 between Raleigh and Wilmington, southeastern North Carolina was booming. I knew there would always be work.

The job was primarily installing heating and air conditioning ductwork. There was not a lot of training involved. It was more like baptism by fire. They would basically hand me a blueprint of the house we were installing a unit in, plus the material for the ductwork, and say, "Here, go put this in."

The more I worked, the more adept I became at the job. I stayed with it a year before deciding to move on to Cape Fear Heating and Air, back across the bridge in Wilmington. I had moved to Leland in order to have a short commute, without having to cross the bridge. Now, I had a new job that had me driving across the bridge anyway, but just in the opposite direction to work. I landed that job in 1988.

Not long into the new job, I received a letter from the licensing board advising me I needed more hours before I could get my HVAC journeyman's card. The time I had worked at Butler's was considered sub-contracting work, so that meant I wasn't getting all the credit for the work I was doing.

I spent almost three years working for Cape Fear Heating and Air. However, I was still just installing units, not repairing them. Fortunately, just before leaving Cape Fear, I did receive my journeyman's status and was overseeing the installations.

Working at Cape Fear became an equivalent to a college education to me. With my desire to read and learn more, I would take the manuals of the units we were installing home and study them after hours. I may not have been working on or repairing the actual units, but I wanted to know how they worked and how to fix them.

My on-my-own education in the HVAC worked went up a notch when I went to work for a well-known heating and air conditioning company in Wilmington – Lewis and Sons. That became a great move for me because they sent me to technical school to learn how to repair certain models of high-efficiency units.

Eventually, word got around about my work. Friends and their friends began to ask me to take a look at their heating and air conditioning systems because they were giving them problems. So, I began to venture out on my own with a bit of freelancing. My boss knew I was taking on some side jobs and told me he had no problem with it.

The way the laws are structured, without a contractor's license in North Carolina, I was not allowed to install a new HVAC system on my own. However, the only thing required to repair them are a business license and an Environmental Protection Agency (EPA) card for the handling of Freon, which is the gas used in many air conditioning systems. Fortunately, many Freon supply houses offer courses on the proper handing of the gas and then administer the course for the card. EPA determined that Freon is hazardous to the environment if not properly handled or discarded with appropriate procedures.

With a business license now in my possession and an EPA card in my wallet, I had a good job and my own side-business, too.

Chapter Seven

I need to back up a little. Not everything in my life was about work at this point. Since the company I ended up working for at the time was located across the Cape Fear River from Wilmington, in Leland, I found a doublewide mobile home in what was a nice community with mostly families. Not too long after moving in, I discovered a friend of mine was having some difficulties. Her name was Rose and I let her move into a spare room in my place. For the first time, I had a roommate.

Life basically fell into a routine. I got up, went to work, came home, ate dinner, relaxed a little and went to bed. At some point, Rose and I grew closer and she developed feelings. However, it never got to a stage where I even considered getting married at that point. It was nice to have her company, though. Not having dated a lot in my past, having a regular someone to spend time with was nice.

The old saying goes there are only three certainties in life, death, taxes and change. I had definitely experienced the taxes and change parts, but didn't know there were significant changes headed my way. They all began in my own neighborhood.

After living in the mobile home community for a while, it became routine, on weekends when the weather was nice, for neighbors to get together and have backyard cookouts to socialize. Rose and I began to participate in some of those and we would sometimes invite neighbors to my place to grill out some burgers, hot dogs or steaks.

The home next to mine had been vacant for a brief period of time before a new family moved in. It was a couple with a little girl. We would exchange neighborly greetings across the yard if we happened to all be outside at the same time.

About six months after they moved in, I invited them over during one of our cookouts and that began a semi-regular series of similar get togethers with our new neighbors.

The wife seemed to be quiet and meek. Her husband obviously was the "man in charge." He seemed a bit controlling to me, but I tried not to judge him. How would I know how he really was with his family? It was easy to see their daughter, who was a little over five years old, was a special needs child. She was sweet, but challenged.

For some time, that was life in my part of the neighborhood. All seemed typical. However, one day that would change.

One Saturday, there was a knock on our door. I answered it to find the neighbor's wife at the door. She seemed very upset and asked if she could talk to my roommate and me. She was taking advantage of the fact her husband had to work this particular Saturday to reach out for help.

We all sat down in my living room and she began to unload. Her husband and her were having serious issues. She said that while he had never been physically abusive to her, he had been emotionally abusive for a long time. In order to hold the family together, she bit her lip and tried to ignore that part.

Things had changed immediately, though. Her daughter had told a teacher in the special education section of her school that her father had molested her. The school was required by law to notify Child Protective Services at the Department of Social Services of the allegation. I was surprised Child Protective Services did not file any claim against the father, they only told Kim she should move out of the residence she shared with her husband to protect her daughter.

Kim reached out to us because she was desperate and at a crossroads. This allegation against her husband could not be overlooked like she had his verbal abuse of her. However, she did not have the resources to go find another place to live.

Rose, my roommate, and I both were surprised Social Services had not more thoroughly investigated the claim made my Kim's special-needs daughter. We thought maybe the authorities believed she was just trying to get her husband in trouble because of the emotional abuse she was suffering. Whatever the case, it was obvious this was a distraught mother who needed help, but found those who were supposed to help shutting the door in her face. Even so-called "Child Protective Services" would not interview her daughter.

Things for my neighbor got worse. Her husband discovered she had contacted law enforcement about their daughter's claim of being molested. Within a few days, he fled the state. His wife eventually learned he had moved in with his mother in Wisconsin. The only thing he had taken with him were some clothes and his car, so it was obvious he was in a hurry to get out of town. No one in our area ever saw him again.

This made problems escalate for my now-abandoned neighbor. While she was glad he was gone and no longer a threat to their daughter or able to verbally abuse her anymore, she did not drive and was left with a challenged daughter to raise on her own. With no income now, she became distraught over what to do.

The home I was renting had two bedrooms, one on each end. There wasn't a great deal of room for two people, much less four, but we realized there was nothing left to do but allow this desperate mom and her daughter to move in when we discovered there was reason to believe the neighbor's husband was molesting their daughter. The little girl was suffering from a learning disability and often had trouble communicating. When things did surface, her mom learned the abuse had possibly been going on since her daughter was about four years old.

I talked everything over with my friend-turned-roommate Rose and we agreed we should let them stay in my home. It seemed the right thing to do. I felt good about being in a position to help her and her daughter during such a difficult time in their lives.

With Rose occupying the extra room in my home, the neighbor, Kim and her daughter, Felicia, slept at night on a pull-out sofa bed in the living room. It wasn't ideal, but Kim seemed very thankful for a place to stay that didn't have the atmosphere of someone belittling her and being a threat to her daughter. With no better choices in her life, Kim and Felicia ended up staying there and things became somewhat normal. That changed when a comment from her daughter to me changed the dynamics, and the living arrangements, in my home.

Chapter Eight

Despite having three roommates now, it wasn't the chaos you'd expect. It definitely wasn't anything like the *Three's Company* TV show from the 70s. Considering three separate situations under the same roof, it became a fairly comfortable arrangement for all of us.

For the next three years, everything remained business as usual, despite the living arrangements. Everyone was getting along well and I felt good to be helping three people. They were a big help to me in return since they prepared most of the meals and kept the place clean. Everything changed when Kim's daughter innocently uttered one word.

Since Felicia had not interacted with her father on a regular basis in a long time, it was understandable she viewed her three years living in my place as her now normal. One day, while all of us were seated in the living room, she came up to me and said, "Daddy, can I have a Mountain Dew?"

That one questioned affected Rose greatly. She had learned she was going to have difficulty having children of her own. Hearing a child refer to me as "Daddy," no matter how innocent, bothered her. I understood why she would be affected by hearing Felicia say that and I also understood why Felicia would think of me in that light. For three years, I was the "man of the house" in her world.

Kim eventually told me she understood why Felicia had begun to see me as "Daddy."

"Considering the atmosphere she had grown up in with my ex-husband, including the verbal abuse and constant belittlement, I understood why Felecia became attached to Mike," Kim said. "Even at that early age, she obviously longed for a father figure who could treat her like a daughter should be treated – with love, kindness, gentleness and respect."

Soon, Rose came to me and said, "I can't do this any longer. I have to go." She moved out leaving just Kim, Felicia and me in the house. Trying to keep things as positive as possible, I was glad to be able to tell Kim she and her daughter could now have the spare bedroom to themselves and not have to sleep on a pull-out couch in the living room. They would have some needed privacy now.

When I told Kim about the change in living arrangements and that she and Felicia would now have their own room, her response came unexpectedly.

"Felicia can sleep in there," she said, pointing to the spare bedroom. Then, pointing at my room, she said, "I can sleep in there."

While I was initially surprised, I was not disappointed. I had begun to have feelings for her and her daughter, but did not want to complicate anything in the home by telling that to anyone or risk making Kim's life anymore difficult than it had already been. Now, my worries had disappeared. When we talked more about this change in our lives, she told me how she felt.

"I've been hoping for a man who would really love me and look out for me," she said. "You took me in, you treated me with respect, you treated my daughter like she was yours and you even took time off from work to help me."

We both decided we would give a relationship a try. It was a try that worked. It has worked ever since, even during two very challenging times in our lives.

Chapter Nine

Life settled into a new routine at my house. Things were going well at work and at home. The relationship between Kim and I was progressing nicely.

The neighborhood was also doing well. The backyard barbeques were continuing to be a regular occurrence. I also found a neighbor I could talk with about a mutual interest.

Most guys during the cookouts talked sports. With all of the university rivalries in the state, there were always long discussions about the games. I was never interested in sports, so I was mostly lost. However, by accident, I discovered one neighbor who had a big interest in computers. Now that was something I could relate to. So, our discussions always centered in technology. By the time he and I had become friends, I was already

Microsoft certified. My interest in computers had begin a long time ago.

I became fascinated in computers when home PCs were uncommon. I went on a quest to learn as much as I could about them. With it being the early stages of home's having computers, courses were hard to find. Today, there is hardly any schools, from elementary through college, where you don't have some kind of access to computer training.

Luckily, I found tons of books at the library and read them all, and this was long before there was even a Windows 98. Initially, I became very interested in networks and troubleshooting them. I also became interested in all aspects of computers from hardware to software and it fascinated me how they all interacted. I built and repaired computers while I was still in high school.

I was even inspired enough to begin a computer set-up and repair business. I opened a shop in a corner of a flea market and offered my services on Fridays, Saturdays and Sundays. That left my weekdays open to search out other opportunities, while still satisfying my computer interests.

It was tempting to choose computers as my career path. However, working on them revealed a part of me that conflicted with working on computers all day. I didn't like to be tied down to one location for hours and days on in. I needed variety. When I saw that HVAC work could give me a variety of places to work in and satisfy my interest in electronics, too, I decided to take that career path. It also was obvious HVAC work was in high demand. Since southeastern North Carolina can be very hot and humid in the summer months and then hover around freezing or below in winter, the work would not be a seasonal situation.

My work in HVAC continued, while my interest in computers would always be there. I had no idea at that time I would make the flip many years later. Lots would happen between the days I talked with my neighbor about technology and the time when computers and the internet would become the main focus of my own company.

Chapter Ten

When I was growing up, my father had taught us all that anything worth having required some work. He didn't have to use those exact words as a lesson, he lived them. So, I knew that even relationships that were good still required sacrifice and hurdles to jump. However, one of the hurdles we would experience seemed to come out of nowhere.

Life for my wife and I became very comfortable. Looking back, I believe the time she and her daughter had just been roommates in my home gave us time to get to know each other and become good friends before a romantic relationship even began. Since that took three years to happen, there weren't many surprises to experience.

Everything naturally progressed into us getting married. Not too long after our wedding, we discovered there would be a new addition to the family. I would soon have a daughter and a step-daughter in the house. We were elated and looking forward to our new daughter. That's when one of those hurdles I talked about came our way. It involved some bizarre laws in North Carolina.

From the time Kim's first husband had left them and fled the state, he had not paid any child support to her. He made it clear he would not pay any child support for a daughter he never saw. I thought that was a convenient excuse he was using. The court process to get her help was a long, drawn out affair. From the time she finally was able to file for support from him, it took four years before she ever received a dime.

Since this began the time she first moved into my home with her daughter, that meant she wasn't able to pay for any rent. I understood that and simply said I was satisfied with all the help they gave me in keeping my place clean and preparing meals. Because of my long work hours, it was a relief to me not to have to do either of the things she was helping me with.

Kim had also attempted to get some help regarding her mentally-challenged daughter. That was slow going, too. Seeing Kim go through the many hoops and delays the government makes people go through to get much needed help really bothered me. Some of these people, like Kim, needed help now, not three years down the road. The system, as I saw it, was broken.

Eventually, after a long period of time, Kim was able to begin receiving some help through the Social Security disability system. That, and child support, was a long time coming.

One part of our situation that helped make our new relationship easier was the fact her mother was supportive and seemed very thankful for me providing a home for her daughter and granddaughter. My wife told me her mom had liked me from the beginning, so that made me feel good. I was glad to hear it because Kim had told me long ago her mother did not like her ex-husband from the get-go. While her mom initially did not know what to think when Kim and Felecia first moved into my home, understandably, as she got to know me and saw Kim living under much less stress, she began to appreciate the situation.

Kim had brothers, but one was a teenager and the other one was around 25 when we became a couple, so they were too busy with their own lives and friends to take too much notice in their older sister's life.

The birth of my own daughter opened a can of worms nobody saw coming. Whether it came because Kim was already in the child support system because of her daughter and ex-husband, or some other way, we found out quite by accident that Kim's divorce to her ex, although filed long before our wedding, had somehow fell through the system and I had not been properly filed. So, in the legal-system's eyes, she was still married to him and not me. The reason this became a huge issue with us is because now, the already flawed child support system, would not acknowledge our marriage, or the fact we lived in the same home. In their one-track mind, I was an "absentee father" and therefore needed to pay child support to my wife. The fact we were together, in the same house, with me providing all of the income for all of us, didn't seem to matter to them.

That wasn't the only legal issue this flaw put us through. Since they did not recognize the flub in the closure of Kim's divorce, they immediately began to list our daughter as her previous husband's child! In my mind, this would be a matter we could quickly resolve.

"That's simple," I told my wife. "I can just take a DNA test and prove I'm the father."

Obviously, what seems simple in anyone's rational mind is not simple when it involves bureaucrats. My request to resolve the issue was completely ignored and I kept getting notices to pay child support. Even more frustrating, I could not get my name placed as father on my own daughter's birth certificate until this was all resolved to the satisfaction of those same bureaucrats.

Until I could get everything straightened out, here I was sending in child support that came right back to our house. In North Carolina, child support is not typically sent directly from the parent required to pay it to the other parent. Instead, it is required to be sent to a state government clearing house where checks are then sent to the parent with custody. If you don't pay it, they simply come arrest you with no questions asked.

Remarkably, it took four years to resolve the whole matter and get the child support fiasco stopped and my name placed on my daughter's birth certificate. Although I had asked more than one judge to review my case, they mostly ignored me and simply assumed the bureaucrats at child support enforcement were automatically right. Plus, although I had proof in my hand, by way of emails and other correspondence I had received from the child support enforcement office that I had complied with providing them all the information and documents to them to make my case, when it was in court they would actually lie and say they had not received the appropriate paperwork from me. I don't think the judge even looked at my documents proving otherwise.

Finally, after reaching that four-year milestone, I found a judge who actually listened to me.

This judge listened intently to what I had to say and the evidence I presented to him. I could tell he was getting a bothersome look on his face. He looked at all the material I gave him, including the address where I lived and the address where Kim's child support payments from me were being sent. I had also had the bailiff take a copy of Kim and I's marriage license to him.

When I had the chance to speak, I asked the judge, "How can the system make me pay child support to a woman I am married to while we all live in the exact same household as husband, wife and daughter?"

The judge finally shook his head and turned to the attorney representing the child support agency. He immediately said he was terminating any requirement I had to pay child support. Not only that, he ordered the child support system to refund all money I had paid through them, plus 20 percent interest!

"He should have never been put into the system in the first place," the judge said. "He deserves that money back and the interest."

In what I assume was either a deliberate action on the child support agency's part or an example of incompetence within the system, it took six months after the judge's order for child support to refund my money and the interest.

This had resolved the child support issue, but there was still the issue regarding paternity of my daughter. We had been told the issue could be quickly resolved by asking Kim's ex-husband to take a paternity test. That frustrated me because I couldn't understand why I couldn't be the one to take the paternity test. Plus, Kim and I both agreed we didn't want to do anything that would place her ex back in contact with Kim or her daughter. We knew it was best and safest for all of us not to involve him at all. As far as we knew, he was still in Wisconsin and the distance was a comfortable one. It was worth the wait. We would learn, though, at a later date, that he had returned to North Carolina and was living in the Winston-Salem area.

Like the child support case, it took that same four years to finally get everything the way it was supposed to be in the first place and have my name placed on my daughter's birth certificate.

Chapter Eleven

For my wife and me, the confrontation with child support people was discouraging. We had both been raised in homes where we were taught to trust our legal system and have respect for all law enforcement personnel. In fact, we had both become fascinated with how the court worked in criminal cases and would occasionally go to the New Hanover County Courthouses to watch trials take place. Now, our own case had left us wondering if the system wasn't broken for some people. We had no idea the big battle we had with the child support people would soon seem like going to traffic court for squeaking through a stop sign, but that would be an experience down the road.

With the paternity and child support issue finally taken care of, we settled into a nice routine. Family life was becoming good for all of us. We began completely enjoying our time together, going to Myrtle Beach for summer vacations and playing Putt-Putt, which we all loved. Holidays had become an all-out family event that brought my family and Kim's family together for great gatherings during Thanksgiving and Christmas.

Felicia was doing well, too. We had signed her into the Special Olympics program and she loved it. She won awards and medals and she was proud of them all and we were proud of her. She also became reacquainted with a friend she had made in middle school. When they both entered high schools, they ended up at different schools. However, when Felicia became a Special Olympics athlete, she found her old friend was in the program, too. They picked up that friendship where they had left off as if they'd never lost contact.

My work was becoming even more productive, too. I had landed a job at a company back "across the bridge" in Wilmington and we moved into the neighborhood where I grew up in the Seagate community. I talked it over with my boss to see if he would mind me going into business for myself, doing some heating and air repair on my own. Wilmington was booming, so my boss didn't see any risk of me competing at all.

Wilmington is still developing fast and the need for heating and air installers and repairmen is always increasing. My interest in electronics had combined with my desire to not be tied down in one location was all being satisfied.

With life now becoming content for all of us, we looked forward to the future. However, life has a tendency to throw something at us when we least expect it. The first of two of these major blows, this one quite was literally a blow in the form of an explosion, happened to me on the job. It would knock out me of commission for a long time.

Chapter Twelve

The accident happened while I was doing repair on a residential HVAC unit. As always, I told the customer not to turn the breaker on to the unit I was working on. Since I was working with exposed wiring on the unit, if the power was on, that could be a very dangerous scenario, and it was.

Thinking he was turning a breaker on for another item in his house, the homeowner accidently turned on the breaker for the HVAC unit. I immediately heard a hum and instinctively covered my face just before the arc from the exposed wiring ignited the oil and refrigerant. The compressor exploded.

Covering my face had protected most of my face, but the rest of me was not so lucky. I realized very quickly I was on fire. Having been involved with the Seagate Fire Department, where my dad was chief, it had been drilled into me to stop, drop and roll. I didn't remember much after dropping and rolling, but regained some consciousness and realized I was holding a water hose, running water on my legs.

Since this was summertime in North Carolina, it was hot, so I was wearing shorts.

Hearing the explosion and looking outside, the lady of the house came running outside.

"Are you okay?"

As often happens when your body is being pumped with adrenalin, I had no idea the real extent of my injuries. I told her, "Oh, I'm fine."

"But, you were just on fire!" she said.

The lady ran back inside and called an ambulance and my boss. When EMTs arrived, they carefully cut my shorts and socks off. They placed me in an ambulance, discussing what treatment I needed.

While I knew the burns were bad, I was focused on the fact it could have been much worse if I had not covered my face and had not dropped and rolled. The training I had from the fire department and hearing my sister, who is a registered nurse, talk about burns, I knew the dos and don'ts of what to do when someone is on fire.

There was definite pain, but I tried not to focus on it. When the EMTs on the scene wanted to give me something right away for the pain, I declined. I had always had a disposition that allowed me to keep my thoughts in check during difficult situations. I have joked that this ability has let me keep a full head of hair, while my brother is, how should I say this, "follically-challenged."

Before I knew it, I was being transferred to the University of North Carolina Burn Center in Chapel Hill. They had requested an air ambulance for me, but there was some bad weather between Wilmington and Chapel Hill, so they transported me by ground.

Not long after arriving at the UNC Hospital Burn Center, I asked a nurse, "How long do you think I'll be here?" I was focused on getting back home and to work.

"You have second and third-degree burns," the nurse said. "So, at least two months, I would guess."

The process of treating burns is very uncomfortable. I highly sympathize and empathize with anyone undergoing the treatment. Around the clock, the nurses have to check and replace the bandages every six hours. They had done the process enough times before to know it was a painful process, so they offered me something for the pain.

"Thanks, but I'm okay. I don't need it."

Just like the EMTs who had arrived at the scene of the HVAC explosion, they looked surprise. The only pain reliever I took while at the burn center was aspirin.

"You can really tolerate some pain," one of the nurses said.

Some of the staff at the burn center also seemed surprised when I turned down something else. I declined their offer to perform skin grafts on my legs. When I heard the procedure would be mainly for cosmetic purposes, I said I didn't want to have the grafts.

"I'm not worried about a scar or two," I told them. "I don't have to look good anymore. I already have a wife."

That was not the only time I had some quips for the burn center staff. At each session to remove and replace the bandages, they would cover my legs with something that looked a lot like Noxzema to me. It was a heavy, very white paste. During one of the bandage sessions, I said, "I need to get some sun. Look how white my legs are."

The nurse I asked about how long I would be in the burn center had mispredicted the length of my stay there. After six days, they sent me home. I had walked out on my own, without a wheelchair. The earlier-than-expected release gave me a false sense of hope I would soon be back to work. However, just because I was out of the hospital didn't mean I was healed.

The fact was I could not stand for more than 15 or 20 minutes without the pain becoming intolerable. The fluid build-up in the areas that were burned made walking and standing too difficult. I had been warned that standing too long allowed the fluid to gather in my lower legs. If I continued to stand for any length of time, that fluid could cause the skin to stretch to the point there would be very loose skin on my legs even after the burned areas healed.

It would be a year before I could return to work. For a guy used to working and paying his own way, it was a big challenge for me to have to step away from work in order to heal. Workman's Compensation did keep us going somewhat, but that was not my idea of making a living.

After getting back home, my wife and I decided it would be more practical for me to initially recuperate at my parent's home. My wife did not drive, so we didn't want to add extra time and effort to my folks to have to come pick me up for the regular doctor visits and the frequent trips I would have to make back to the UNC Hospital Burn Center. Another factor was my mother. She was a natural worrier, so she would have likely been at our home 24/7 anyway.

Being mostly stuck at home during that year was an enormous challenge. This was before the internet was common in everyone's home, so spending time on social media or binge-watching Netflix or YouTube videos was not an option. I spent most days reading the newspaper and watching some TV. Slowly, but surely, the healing finally made it to a point I was able to return to work. I never wanted to be in a situation where I was not able to provide for my family again.

It took some time, but I was able to get back to work and begin to live on a real income instead of depending on Workman's Compensation payments. Plus, my sideline business had grown into fulltime one, so I told my boss I was ready to go on my own. Not only did he understand, he said he would hire me to do work as a subcontractor for him during his busy months. I was officially working for myself and Powlas Enterprises was now a full-fledged company.

I know lots of people in the HVAC world who run large companies with lots of employees. In the traditional business sense, they are very successful. However, I noticed they never had time to spend with their families. I decided I would mostly be a one-man band. I didn't want the headaches and responsibility of a very large operation. I said many times, "I want to make a livin', not a killin.'"

Again, I was entering a cycle where work and family life were getting back to normal.

Speaking of family life, our little family had added an addition, a son named after me. We were now a family of five. Everyone was doing well, and Felicia was enjoying her roll as "big sister." She even taught our daughter, Hope, to walk. I never considered or treated Felicia as anyone other than one of our three children. I was very careful to never show partiality to the other two simply because they were "my" children.

The crazy business we had experienced with child support regarding our daughter and the issue with her birth certificate had thankfully become ancient history to us. However, I would still occasionally think how bizarre the laws could be. Little did I know I would discover not only how bizarre laws could be, but how disturbing and powerful the legal system could be.

Chapter Thirteen

My stepdaughter, Felicia, entered high school under a special program and had become closer friends with a girl she had met in Middle School, thanks to their involvement in Special Olympics. They began to have sleepovers to spend time together on weekends. Before we knew it, Felicia had turned 17 years old.

For some reason we never have figured out, Felicia's friend had a father who did not like me. Since he had at one time worked for the same company I did, I wondered if he was resentful I was doing well working for the company and the boss being okay with me having my own side business. I don't know, but Kim and I certainly didn't want something we didn't understand to keep Felicia from spending time with a friend she really liked.

There was an agency similar to Big Brother/Big Sister that served special needs children. Felicia and her friend belonged to the group and they would have outings together. That gave them more time to socialize. We knew that was good for both of them.

During a sleepover at her friend's house, Felicia apparently told her friend about the incident that had happened when she was about five years old involving her biological father. In relaying the story, she said, "Daddy touched me."

Apparently, Felicia's friend's parents overheard part of the conversation. While we believe they already knew about the incident when Felicia was young, they overacted and instantly assumed she was talking about me. They did not know Felicia routinely referred both to her biological father and me as "Daddy." So, they instantly placed the blame on me. Then, all hell broke loose.

Chapter Fourteen

Without Kim, nor I, having a clue what was going on, the parents of Felicia's friend called Social Services, who in turn contacted law enforcement.

One day, while we were all at home, there was a knock on the door. When my wife and I went to the door, we found two people, who identified themselves as being with Child Protective Services. They were accompanied by a law enforcement officer with papers in his hand. They were an order for Felicia to be immediately removed from our house.

"Felicia is moving out," one of the CPS workers said, curtly.

With that, they came inside, took Felicia and left. I was in shock and my wife was instantly and understandably a basket case. We had tried to ask CPS why they were taking Felicia and they ignored us. We had heard news stories about the power of Child Support Enforcement, but never thought, in a million years, that power would be unleashed on our family.

We didn't know what was going on, but knew something was obviously up. Was her biological father back in the picture? Had he obtained some order under false pretenses? We had no idea. No one would tell Kim or me anything. Our answer came a few days after they had taken Felicia.

Because of the situation we were in, my sister came over frequently to give Kim some moral support. She was there visiting us when another six vehicles, including vans and a police car, pulled into the yard. When we came to the door, they put me in handcuffs and sent in people from the van into the house. They presented my wife and my sister with a search warrant and started removing items out of the house. They found six computers in my collection, some I was simply working on, and loaded them into the van along with some other items.

Finally, they told me what I was being arrested for. They said I was being charged with molesting Felicia and all of the secondary charges that came with that. When my wife heard the charges, she went ballistic. She began attempting to tell them who had really committed the act, but they had no interest in listening They were like a pack of dogs circling and barking not only up the wrong tree, but the wrong neighborhood.

My wife became even more upset when they would not allow my sister to take our son and daughter somewhere so they would not be home going through the horror of seeing their father arrested and items being taken out of their house. She made her concerns about the potential life-long affect that would have on our children, but the officers ignored her and still demanded the children remain.

Looking back, I now believe the officer's ignored Kim because they had convinced themselves she "knew" I had committed the crime and she was just covering up for me so she would have a breadwinner in the house. That was a ridiculous assumption.

I did not want to make my wife more upset by overreacting, so I remained as calm as possible. I'm sure they expected the cries of "I didn't do anything!" like they most likely hear on a routine basis. Instead, I turned to Kim and said, "Honey, we'll just have to let this take it's course. It will be okay and the truth will come out."

With that, they took me and placed me into the back of the police car while the other people loaded up my computers and what they thought might be evidence into the vans I sat quietly in the back of the police car thinking it would be just a matter of a little time to straighten the whole mess out and see they had arrested the wrong guy. I think the officers were surprised at my demeanor, considering they were taking items out of my house. I assume they were convinced they would find child pornography or some other evidence to back up their case. I wasn't concerned at all. I knew what data was on my computers. It was almost all work-related.

If we thought the Child Support enforcement people had been ridiculous in taking so long to resolve the issue of my own daughter, that would seem nothing compared to what I was heading into on the ride in the back of a police car to a police station to be questioned. What respect I had for the legal system would soon change dramatically. I had grown up hearing our rights of being innocent until proven guilty. But, I didn't know that the reality was you could be treated guilty no matter how innocent you were.

Chapter Fifteen

The police took me to a new police station that had been built in Wilmington. Still in handcuffs, they took me inside and to a room where detectives began questioning me. At one point one of them asked, "You want a lawyer."

"No, I don't have anything to hide," I said. "Ask me anything you want."

While I understand detectives have all kinds of tactics and games they play in an interrogation process, it was a very frustrating experience for me to be sitting across from them and knowing completely well they were the ones not being honest. That was obvious when one of them blurted out a statement.

"We have enough testimony to hold you," he said.

They had zero interest in hearing me explain the confusion or give them the facts regarding Felicia's biological father.

For them, this was now a chess match and they intended to win. While I was frustrated, I could tell it was driving them crazy I would not just confess.

After they got through a long period of time in their attempts to force me into saying I had done something I did not do, I calmly replied, "It will all come out and you'll see I'm not the one who did this."

Just as they were convinced I was the one who did do it, I'm sure they were chomping at the bit to get forensics back on the six computers they seized from my house. I have no doubts they thought they'd find all kinds of "bad stuff" on them. Boy, were they in for a surprise, but it would take a long, long time for them to admit it.

Chapter Sixteen

After a long interrogation at the police station, I was transported to the New Hanover County Jail. I was being held until a bond hearing.

Because of the seriousness of the charges, as well as the fact prisoners are often violent with those accused of crimes against a child, I was placed inside a maximum security unit. The door was not like one you typically see on TV shows about jail. This one had a solid door with a small, sliding door they could slide food and other supplies into. It is a depressing, overwhelming experience to be placed inside and hear that door shut.

I tried to maintain a positive attitude. Knowing I was innocent helped. Plus, I was sure the bond hearing would result in me being able to be released so that I could return home until a trial date could be set and I would be exonerated of any charges. That was not to happen on the timeline I hoped it would.

Since I had lost income, I was appointed a court-appointed attorney. At the bond hearing, the attorney argued I had never had any trouble with the law before. In fact, I only had one traffic ticket on my record and that was for windows tinted too darkly in a car I had bought. I had not been the one to install the tint in the first place.

My attorney and I were both stunned when the judge, who had obviously ignored any of the evidence my attorney had presented, and who was likely single-mindedly focused on the seriousness of the accusation, set my bond at $500,000. I knew my family did not have the resources to post a bond with such a high amount. I had to accept the fact I wasn't going home.

The amount of the bail made no sense to me. When my wife and I had an interest in some of the trials taking place at the courthouse, quite a while before I would find myself as one of the ones being accused, we saw very serious repeat offenders regularly got $20,000 or $30,000 bonds. So, I kept thinking, where did half-a-million dollars come from? I guess when Child Protective Services and police team up on you, there goes the bail elevator up, whether the charges are justified or not.

That was not the first hard punch to the gut I would get from the legal system. The other came when I discovered Social services has succeeded in getting a judge to sign an order prohibiting me from having any contact with my own son and daughter. I could not call them or write them. That was very disturbing to me. I could somewhat understand an order prohibiting contact with my stepdaughter Felicia until the case was resolved, but no evidence existed that would in any way indicate it was not in my children's best interest to have contact with their father. I was still trying to keep the faith, but I had to bite my tongue on that one.

Despite the high bond and order to not have contact with my son and daughter, I tried my best to keep the faith. I knew this would eventually be resolved. Instead of focusing on my own troubles, I kept Kim in mind hoping she was okay. I knew she was under an extreme amount of stress. With her suffering from frequent migraine headaches, I was worried how she was holding up. She was dealing not only with a daughter jerked from her home and a husband taken to jail, but also with an instant loss of any household income.

It took me about two or three months of being in jail to grasp just how the system worked for those of us on the inside. No one sat us down and said, you can do this during these times and these other things during these other times. We had to almost figure out on our own how we could make phone calls home or how we could buy any supplies we might need inside the jail.

Lights in the jail came on at 6:00 a.m. Then, sometime between 6:00 and 7:00 we would be served breakfast. Remember, I was placed in a maximum security cell and that meant I did not go eat with the other prisoners. They slid my meal into me through that small sliding door that was part of the large solid door. It was a demoralizing experience, but I focused on being in there as much for my protection as for anyone else's. I also kept telling myself, this won't be long.

Between 10:00 and 11:00 a.m., or from 2:00 until 3:00 p.m., we had what was called "rec time." The inmates were allowed to leave their cell and walk around inside the jail for little exercise or watch a centrally-located television. You could also take a shower during rec time. All of this happened indoors. The only time I ever saw daylight from outside was when I was transported from the jail to the courthouse for a hearing.

On the outside, my wife was becoming very depressed, No one within the system would tell her anything. Plus, detectives were also interviewing her in an attempt to "break her" and have her admit she "knew what I had done" and was just trying to cover up for me. I was telling her all the updates when I talked to her by phone, but I'm sure she wondered if my versions were just attempts to make her feel better.

In addition to having a husband in jail for something she knew he didn't do, she had had her oldest daughter taken away and was not allowed any contact with her. To make matters much worse, she was left with two children and the stress of trying to keep a household going with an almost non-existent income. She had begun receiving a monthly stipend from the

Social Security disability system because of our son's health challenges. However, that was nowhere near enough to even cover basic living expenses.

Family on both sides, especially my father, helped as much as they could. My dad made sure the light bill was paid and he frequently brought groceries to Kim. He also paid for medication prescribed for our son and for Kim. Despite that help, none of my family was Bill Gates, so there was a limit to what anyone could do.

My wife and I had spent 11 years building a life and some security together only for her to see all of that taken away in the back of a police car.

Chapter Seventeen

During a meeting with my attorney at the prison, he again talked about how shocked he was over the $500,000 bond. He scheduled a hearing in court to have it reduced.

The hearing for the bond reduction was practically a repeat of my first court appearance. My attorney had told me, "You have no record at all and they don't have enough evidence for this."

Again, we were both surprised when the judge denied the motion to reduce my bail even one dollar. It revealed to me the enormous power of certain charges, especially one involving a child. Just an accusation of committing such a crime can bring a "you're guilty" response no matter what the facts were. The power of Child Protective Services was again on display. I believe all children need protection and appreciate CPS when they really do intervene in terrible situations. But, this was a case, and I wondered how many more there were, where they got it wrong and their power was misspent.

I had heard child molestation was a charge frequently used in custody hearings. In fact, some lawyers tell clients in nasty custody cases, "Just wait, they'll accuse you of some sexual thing before this is all over with."

Some judges are very aware of this, but this wasn't a custody case, so I believe the judge wasn't on the same level of vigilance they would have been in family court cases. Whatever the reason, it appeared the court's attitude was, "We're not sure if he's guilty or not, so let's not take any chances and just keep him behind bars."

When I was taken back to the jail after the hearing, I had the tough job of having to call my wife and tell her a bond reduction had been denied. She did not drive and had the challenge of taking care of our two children by herself, so I discouraged her from trying to go to the trouble of attending any court hearings I had. When I filled her in, she was in the same shock I was in. However, I tried very hard not to show any serious disappointment. I didn't want to upset her any more than she already was. I knew showing any anger or fear on my part, would only make things worse, so I was careful what I said to Kim.

"It's okay, because in the end I'm going to win this," I told her.

Chapter Eighteen

At the same time my wife had to depend on me entirely for any news on my case, I was also in the dark regarding everything she was experiencing on the outside.

During a discussion, a representative from the District Attorney's office was having with me and my attorney, he actually told me my wife was in the process of ending her relationship with me and was going to file for divorce. I knew that was a lie, but it was disgusting me how low they would go in thinking that would wrangle some kind of confession out of me since I would think there was no reason to want to go home.

At a later meeting with a deputy district attorney, they had put together a plea deal and placed it before my attorney and me. It would reduce the charge to "assault and battery on a female" if I signed a confession to that charge.

"If you think I'm guilty of doing what you said I did to my stepdaughter, why would you even offer me this," I told them.

The district attorney's rep replied, "We are just trying to be nice."

I responded to that with, "I'm not going to be in here much longer."

After they left, my attorney and I were on the same wavelength. We knew what the DA said was a lie. We also knew this meant they didn't have any real evidence, other than the misguided testimony of the couple who were the parents of Felicia's friend.

Here's where people hearing my story become shocked. This plea deal came after they had been holding me, without any kind of a real trial, for over a year. The decline in my respect for the legal system dropped even more when they retaliated against my attorney and me by dragging things out even longer. It was simply arrogance at work.

For most of that year, there was another issue dragging my case out in addition to the district attorney's actions. My original attorney was just not putting any serious effort into my case. I've heard stories before of some attorneys being in no hurry to resolve a case because they are getting paid on a regular basis. So, where's the motivation. Yet another flaw I saw in the system.

It would take a while, but a little bravery on my part would land me with an attorney who hit the ground running in my case. She was the one who was in the meeting with the DA when they offered the plea deal. Even their attempt to make that offer showed me they knew she was not going to drag out this case any longer than necessary to get it resolved once and for all.

However, during that year before she became part of my case and the time until she could have success in finally getting my case resolved, I had to continue surviving mentally while I waited the over 500 days they would end up holding me. I read a lot. I also delved back into the Bible. I took courses on the Bible that would lead to me becoming an ordained minister after I was eventually released. In addition, I did make a few friends in the jail and that gave us people to talk to.

Despite the frustration regarding my case, I was very fortunate to be able to keep an even keel. In fact, it wasn't unusual for some guards to think I might be going into a depression.

One guard, after asking me if I was okay said, "You're acting like you're not in here."

"It's the way I was raised," I said to the guard. "My mother always said, 'If you're innocent, stick with it.' Well, I'm innocent."

While my demeanor and attitude helped, I don't want to give the impression I was fine spending every day and night, except for two hours a day, in a concrete-walled, eight-by-fourteen room with a bunk, a small sink and a small window. It did take a toll. Remember, I was the guy who chose the HVAC field because I didn't want to be confined to one area for a long period of time.

On some occasions, I would be confined to the cell 24 hours, up to a week at a time. That happened when another inmate misbehaved or created problems. It was common practice for all of us to be punished for the actions of one or two other inmates. It gave a whole new meaning to the old cliché, "One bad apple can spoil the whole bunch."

A big contributing factor helping both Kim and me maintain our sanity would be courtesy of the U.S. Postal Service. I began doing something rarely done these days. I wrote my wife letters almost every day and she would write me back as often as she could, considering all she was going through on the outside.

Kim was definitely taking the biggest hit to me being in jail. With all of the pressure of trying to take care of two children with more income that always ran out at the end of the month began taking a serious toll on her. As the month's dragged on, she was losing any hope that I would be released anytime soon at all. Finally, her depression hit so hard she knew she could not function as a mother for a while, so our two children were placed in the Boys and Girls Home of North Carolina in Lake Waccamaw for a little over four months. Hearing that was tough on me. I can only imagine how difficult that decision was on Kim.

I kept hoping my letters would help. We were able to talk on the phone on a regular basis, but a letter was something we could pick up and read over again during those times we couldn't talk.

Chapter Nineteen

Knowing Kim was dealing with so many challenges while I sat and waited in the New Hanover County Jail, I tried to make my letters home appear to be as normal as possible. I wanted her to know she didn't need to add any worries about how I was handling things to the long list of what she was having to deal with at home.

As I mentioned, I wrote home every day. I certainly hoped it helped Kim deal with the dark days, but it was also great therapy for me. As I wrote home and asked about her and the children or gave her messages to pass along to my son and daughter, it helped me visualize my family. That helped a lot. It gave me something to look forward to almost every day, a kind of normalcy in the chaos.

Occasionally, I would use the letters to ask for a little help, such as getting some money sent so I could buy supplies and a radio to help break the boring times. I had figured out how to have items like that sent to me.

As the letters were exchanged and we had our frequent phone chats, the more time clicked by, the more difficult things were for Kim. She had resorted to staying inside with the doors locked. When she reached the stage of turning our son and daughter over to someone else's care, she came very close to giving up. She even stopped taking the medicine her doctor had prescribed.

I felt better when I learned a friend intervened and took her into her home to give her some much-needed moral support. However, I knew it was going to take a miracle to get my family back together into some kind of normalcy after this nightmare. However, I believe in miracles and one was coming my way. Not as fast as I had hoped, but it was coming.

Chapter Twenty

THE LETTERS

To see how we communicated, here are many of the letters we exchanged during my days waiting for my case to finally be resolved. Most of the letters were much longer than what I share here.

> Oct 19, 2010
>
> Dear Kim,
>
> I love you.
>
> Hope we get to see each other today. Where has this year gone?
>
> They still haven't fixed the AC in here. They say it will be 80 today, but the AC runs all the time, so we just have to stay covered up.

Knowing I will be coming home soon makes it better in here for me. So, it is nothing but a little time in a cold temperature.

I hope they let you see me today. Maybe the one at the desk will have a soft heart and let you through this time.

Well, looks like they would not let you visit. I will have to put you on the list for Tuesday.

Love,
Daddy & Husband Mike

Dec. 6, 2010

Dear Kim,

It is almost time for lunch. Hope it will be good and warm like breakfast was.

Hope you got the tree put up. We will have our Christmas when I come home, so keep the tree up until I get there.

I have been reading *Decision Points* by George W. Bush. It is only 720 pages, so it should not take long to read.

Code Red must be over with since they are letting the guys out now.

Remember, I love you all very much and working on my way back to you.

Love always,
Daddy & Husband Mike

Dec 8, 2010

Dear Kim,

I will call you every time I get out at 7 or 9, no matter what. I know how much you and the kids love me calling.

You and the kids are the family God has given me and I will fight to the end to keep it that way, no matter what.

Well, on the coldest morning, they forgot to send coffee to us. Thank goodness I have back-up. I only have two left after this one. Boy, it is cool in here this morning.

Love always,
Daddy and Husband Mike

Dec. 24, 2010

Dear Kim,

It is 10:00 a.m. and we just got back in from our rec time. Wish I was there to help you put all the gifts under the tree for our kids this year. We will make up for the days we missed apart.

I cannot believe Junior will be in middle school next year. Time has gone by so fast.

I will write more on Saturday. Until then, good night. I love you all very much.

Needless to say, despite the hopes I expressed in the letters to Kim, I would not be coming home as soon as I thought. Knowing I was innocent, I trusted the system would discover the error in arresting me and would release me. My trust would continue to wane as a new year began, but I kept the letters going home to my wife and my children.

> Jan. 3, 2011
>
> Hello Kids,
>
> Daddy loves you. Do what Mom asks you to do.
>
> I will be home soon so we can go outside to play with your new toys and ride bikes.
>
> Love,
> Daddy

At the time I wrote that note to my children, I had no idea it would be after another Christmas before I would return home.

Chapter Twenty-One

It wasn't easy trying to be a father from a distance, but I tried by sending encouraging messages inside letters to Kim. I also tried to encourage her as best I could. She was dealing with incredible stresses. I wasn't concerned about what I was going through, but was incredibly worried about how this all was affecting my family.

> Jan. 5, 2011
>
> P.S. Mike, Jr., Keep up the good work in school, OK? Daddy loves you!

Jan. 11, 2011

Dear Kim,

How do the kids like all the snow we have been having? I hear they got two days off from school. I'm sure you're loving that!
LOL

I cannot wait to get out of here to get back to you and the kids. Plus, I want to get back to work. This is the longest I have not worked for the last 20-something years.

Well, rec time is over, so I will finish up and get to bed for the night. Stay warm
and get better.

Love,
Daddy and Husband Mike

I had begun a new year still in the New Hanover County Jail, still pondering how I could be kept this long. I focused on knowing the truth would have to come out and I would be released any day. However, that wasn't happening. Months went by. While I stayed positive, the frustration increased. The letters home, plus the phone calls to Kim, kept me going.

June 27, 2011

Dearest Kim,

Still, nothing has changed, but hope we will get some good news soon.

How has it been with the kids being out of school? Have you had other kids over much?

Let Hope know that Daddy is proud of her going into the 8th grade. I love Junior's photo that you sent. He is getting so big!

Nothing means more to me than our love, our home and our family. The so-called little things we do together, the day-to-day moments we spend together, add up to a life that is satisfying, meaningful and good.

Keep the prayers going. Keep the letters coming.

Love always,
Mike

July 4, 2011

How are my wonderful wife and kids doing this 4th of July? So many things we would be doing if I was there with you – out to eat, fireworks, Carolina Beach, 4 X 4, and Britt's Donuts.

I'm glad the weather is nice so we can go outside for fresh air. I hate part of our rec room. We can't even see any trees or walk on grass. It's just a room with four walls about 25 feet high and no roof.

Until the next letter, keep up the good work, write when you can, stop by when you can, keep the prayers going and look for me soon to be back home with you three.

Love always & forever,
Mike

As you can see, I never dwelled too much on what was happening at the jail, just enough to let Kim know things were not luxurious, but I was staying positive. The goal was to be as normal as possible in a situation that was anything but normal. I had made a friend in the jail by the name of Lewis. On occasion, he was the source of some humor I could share with Kim, as I mentioned in a letter I sent home before I spent the first Christmas in jail.

> Oct. 31, 2010
>
> It is 8:00 a.m. and we have hot water again. I did not take a shower yesterday since there was no hot water. Lewis forgot and got into the shower anyway. He had a few words to say when he turned on the water. I don't think it would be called singing in the shower.

I wrote home almost every day, but Kim was only able to respond when she could. I loved getting letters from home when she was able to write, but I completely understood why she could write me back every time she got a letter from me. She was dealing with more than any human should have to back home.

Chapter Twenty-Two

As a year passed during my time being held in jail, information was still hard to come by for Kim and me. I learned that the order preventing Kim from communicating with Felicia also included no contact between Felicia and her half brother and sister. That was disturbing to me.

We also learned Felicia had been initially placed with the parents of her friend that had created this wrongful accusation in the first place. I was glad she was with someone she knew and liked, as far as her friend was concerned, while it still bothered me she was under the care of her friend's parents. Later on, Felicia would be removed from that home, too, and placed in a group home facility.

As far as my case was concerned, I was growing frustrated over my attorney's lack of progress in getting me an actual trial.

Whatever happened to the right to a "speedy" trial?

Occasional motions were being made in my case, but an actual trial had not been scheduled. During one of those motions, I got brave and asked the judge if I could address the court. He agreed. I mentioned my concern over the slow movement on the case. I also mentioned the poor communication and unreturned phone calls from my attorney. I asked if another attorney could be assigned to me.

I was happily surprised when the judge agreed and appointed another attorney, a lady, to my case. My decision to ask the judge for a new attorney would be a good one. She hit the ground running, even to the point of greatly annoying the district attorney's office. She would accomplish significantly more in a few months than my previous attorney had in over a year.

My new attorney began meeting with me twice a month to share and gather details on my case. She also met with Kim to see if her actual story was what the district attorney's office was claiming. I also found out she was frequently on the phone with the district attorney requesting they provide her with any evidence they had. When the DA ignored her request, my attorney filed a motion with the court demanding they release any and all evidence and forensics they had in my case.

"Do you mind going to court if I file these motions?" my attorney asked.

"Not at all," I said. "Throw everything you can at them."

It wasn't long after that filing, the DA showed up with the plea deal I mentioned earlier. It was obvious my lawyer was building a fire in their office.

The work my attorney was accomplishing created a situation where I was more frequently being transported by van to the New Hanover County Courthouse for hearings. My attorney had come on board during the summer, so from July until December, I was becoming a regular visitor to court.

Some of the motions my attorney filed were dismissed, but some were not. Even when a motion was dismissed, it didn't affect me too much because at least this attorney was aggressively pursuing an end to my case.

I had begun to get transported between the jail and the courthouse so often I actually develop a kind of friendship with courthouse personnel.

Some of the hearings on the motions technically could be handled by my attorney without me having to attend the hearing. In fact, on one occasion when the van arrived at the courthouse carrying me for a hearing, a bailiff came to the van and said, "You don't have to be here, your attorney has already handled the motion."

I had the right to be at any hearing involving my case, so I took advantage to go to them all, whether it was required or not. It gave me a chance to get out of the jail and to eat a better meal at the courthouse.

Once, during the slew of motions my attorney was filing, the judge addressed me directly.

"I've seen you what, five times in the past several months? Yet, you're always smiling even though you know how serious the charges are," the judge said.

"That's because I know I'm innocent and you have the wrong guy," I said.

One of the motions my attorney filed would have a significant impact on my case and anger the DA's office, too, putting them in retaliation mode.

Chapter Twenty-Three

My attorney filed a motion to compel the district attorney's office to release any evidence that had against me, including any and all forensics, including from the six computers they had seized from my home. My attorney was getting aggravated that I had been held for over a year at this point and there had been no actual trial calendared by the DA.

When the hearing on that motion was held, the judge sided with us, big time. He seemed angry at the DA's handling of my case and ordered them to give my attorney all evidence within 30 days or he would have them held in contempt of court. He spent at least ten minutes chastising the deputy DA for their poor handling of my case. You could tell that made the prosecutor mad. They went on a retaliation spree trying to find anything they could to file additional charges against me.

Before those 30 days were up, the district attorney filed a motion for me to be held accountable on two worthless check charges. I had goofed when I was 19 years old and accidently wrote two checks for under $20.00 each. That had happened over a decade ago. They also tried to make it look like I was some kind of "repeat offender" by mentioning I had received a traffic ticket for windows being too heavily tinted in a used car had purchased years ago. The car came like that and I wasn't the one who had tinting done in the first place.

When a hearing was scheduled on that case, my attorney had those charges dismissed before the jail van could get me to the courthouse. The worthless check charges were dismissed for being outside the statue of limitations in the first place.

Both my attorney and I read between the lines of that motion in particular. They had no real evidence against me and they were grasping at straws to retaliate. That's when they offered the plea deal I already mentioned. I knew my case was finally coming to a head, but it still didn't happen overnight.

When the 30 days were approaching in my attorney's motion compelling the DA's office to release the evidence and forensics in my case, the attorney met with me to discuss what they had provided. That happened in June.

In July, during a meeting with my attorney about what the DA had provided, she said, "They're going to have to come up with something phenomenal for them to be successful prosecuting this case."

It appeared all the evidence they had was hearsay. My attorney immediately had that evidence thrown out and was successful. That left them with nothing. The forensics had produced nothing, including on my computers.

That was when the charges of the checks and the window tinting came out if nowhere for them to have an excuse to hold me at least another 30 days so they could keep trying to find something against me. It would all fail, but those wheels of justice seemed to be going uphill at a time I thought this would be over any minute. However, my attorney had to play the games with the DA.

Finally, after all the court maneuvering had taken place, my attorney filed the big one, a motion to have all charges against me dismissed.

That final motion came around late October. I had been held in the New Hanover County Jail for well over a year with no actual trial on my charges. Since any motions came with an automatic 30-day response period, along with time it would take my attorney to go over their filed response to our motion, my hope of being out for the upcoming holidays was dwindling.

The timing would have meant a hearing could have been placed on the calendar around a week before Christmas. However, the courthouse becomes practically a ghost town from a period about the week before Christmas until after the first week in January. So, I was back in wait mode. I held on to the hope this would all come to a head and the new year would be a good one. I was desperate to re-unite my family and rebuild my business as soon as I was released.

Chapter Twenty-Four

My attorney had my case placed on the calendar for January 20th, 2012. I arrived by way of the jail van and found my attorney ready to go. She had stacks of papers in front of her ready to counter any claims the district attorney's office had left.

During the meetings between the time the DA's office had been ordered to release the evidence and forensics in my case, my attorney and I had several meetings at the courthouse creating a response to everything they claimed. She was very detailed. She would tell me a claim they had made and I would respond to it in detail.

Since we had filed the court date, my attorney was allowed to present her case first. She was confident in addressing the judge.

She emphasized the fact I had been held in jail for a year and a half with no real evidence from the district attorney, except poor hearsay evidence the court had already determined was not admissible. She also strongly made the point my wife and children were suffering greatly during my absence that was the fault of the DA's unsubstantiated claims.

Even though the check case had been dismissed, my attorney held up a piece of paper to make a point to the judge.

"This is his record, your honor," she said. "Two checks written more than a decade ago for under $20 each."

My lawyer also mentioned the $500,000 bail and how that had been applied by another judge and that amount was significantly higher than many who had been charged with taking another's life.

She went through every aspect of the case and finally made her closing argument.

"Your honor, justice is for this man to go home, unless the district attorney can show some kind of evidence he committed this crime. It's been a year and a half and they've presented nothing."

Finally, she even hinted at a civil lawsuit of I wasn't released.

With so many details going back and forth, the judge did not give a final ruling in the case. That would take about two more weeks.

A few days before the end of January, my attorney came to see me in the jail. She wanted to deliver the news in person. My case and all of the charges had been completely dismissed by the judge. There was still a day or two of final, official paperwork to be filed so the jail could release me.

On January 31st, my attorney came by to say the paperwork had been completed and I was being released later that day. However, as if to get one final dig in retaliation, the DA's office did not send the official order over until the next day. I thought that was a childish action on their part and further enhanced my worries about how dangerous unchecked power could be.

Chapter Twenty-Five

February 1st, 2012, I walked out of the New Hanover County Jail a free man. I had spent 513 days being held for a crime I did not commit based on misdirected hearsay evidence that would have never held up.

Believe it or not, I wasn't angry. I don't get angry easily. I was, though, disgusted and disappointed. Disgusted on how easily people's lives could be destroyed by a powerful system. I was disgusted mainly over how this had affected my family. My wife had suffered to the point of a nervous breakdown, forcing my children into a children's home for over four months, and this was after she had already had her daughter stripped from our house.

My disappointment was based on how my wife and I had both been raised in a home where we praised America and had complete faith in the legal system. Despite the fact most people are guilty of crimes in which they are charged, it never occurred to me it was possible for me to ever experience being in the category of those who were wrongfully accused of a crime they truly did not commit. Since my release, my radar is always up when I hear someone has been released after spending most of their life behind bars only to have a new set of eyes from a non-profit group that now looks for cases that are flawed. Compared to some of those cases, my 513 days being wrongfully held seems trivial.

The process to get me cleared and released should be a textbook example of how not to run our courts. I had sadly learned, firsthand, at the expense of my family and me, the system is seriously flawed. No one should have to go through this.

There was a brief moment of personal humor for me during the process of being released. It involved the computers they had seized at my home the day of my arrest.

As I was going through the process of being released, I was asked if I wanted the computers they had seized during my arrest to be returned to me.

"No, I don't want something the DA went through and most likely destroyed. Besides, I still have all the same data that was on the computers on a back-up hard drive at home they didn't take," I said.

I did not want to waste time revisiting the past and dwelling on being wrongfully accused and jailed for that long. My entire focus quickly became trying to recreate some kind of normal life back home.

Within 48 hours after being released, I was on the phone and creating advertising to rebuild my HVAC service business. I wanted to bring financial security back into my wife's life and bring sanity back to my family.

Chapter Twenty-Six

It would not be an overnight situation, but slowly Kim and I began putting our lives back together. With our two children now back home, we started to feel like an intact family again.

Plus, my HVAC business was growing again. Thankfully, the internet helped. I listed my business on sites that homeowners turned to for recommendations and reviews of people and companies who did any home repair, maintenance and other work. Powlas Enterprises was back in business.

In any business, some months are better than others. Because of the challenges my wife had been through while I was in jail, any month that even looked like there would be more month than money made her nervous. I understood that and assured her we would make it through those months and we did.

Since I hit the ground running when I was released, it didn't take too long to put the business well back into the black. With constant development going on in Wilmington, there was still no shortage of work. I had rebuilt my reputation. In addition to word-of-mouth advertising, the ads I placed online through sites like HomeAdvisor were paying off.

The more I saw the success of advertising online, the more my interest in computers was being rekindled. I realized placing video content on YouTube, showing how HVAC systems worked and common problems with them, would set me apart as more of a specialist in the field. It worked. I saw the value of YouTube and a presence online.

My brain began some serious storming. I knew if YouTube and other online sites could expand my business, imagine what it could do for other entrepreneurs. After spending several years successfully rebuilding my HVAC business, I felt a huge shift coming my way and the internet would be a huge part of it.

Chapter Twenty-Seven

YouTubers, as they had become to be known, have quite a community. They are using the site to promote their work or themselves, but they are always wanting to learn more about how to make the use of the site more effective. So, they create regional events where those who have successfully used the site can offer advice and ideas to those who are new to the process.

Even experienced YouTube users understand the constant change happening in the online world, so attending these events had grown into a huge information exchange opportunity. Soon, I was invited to not only attend these events, but to make presentations. While it took a while, it almost seemed I had become a YouTube expert overnight. I enjoyed sharing what I had learned and I also enjoyed the camaraderie.

Before we knew it, Kim and I were traveling across the country to attend and participate in the YouTube events. Since our children were old enough to be on their own, it was as if we were going on a series of honeymoons we never had.

Kim was not interested in flying, so we traveled by car or bus to the events. Going to the west coast events were long commutes, but it gave us a chance to see America. We enjoyed the adventure of traveling.

To this day, I still utilize YouTube for my business and offer consulting services for others wanting to efficiently utilize the site successfully. My old interest in technology had come full circle and it was becoming much more of a part of my business than my HVAC work. In fact, another technology-based business would lead to me putting my HVAC business to the side.

Wilmington had been the town Kim and I both had grown up in, but it was changing fast. The growth was creating traffic nightmares and it was not the city with a small town feel it used to be. When Kim and I had the opportunity to move to a little more rural area in Onslow County, about 50 miles north of Wilmington, we took it.

Once we were settled into our new home, I began to hear story after story of people having problems getting broadband internet service. That wasn't an issue around cities like Wilmington, but you didn't have to travel far to discover there were thousands of people who could not get much more than slower DSL service. Some tried satellite-based internet access, but had issues with it, especially during bad weather, which is when you need it the most.

The more I heard of underserved areas, the more I wanted to help. My research quickly introduced me to a system known as Wireless Internet Service Provider, referred to in the industry as WISP.

The system uses existing digital access through cell towers and creates localized wireless internet access using a specialized antenna. If that antenna is placed on a high-enough tower, it's possible to provide internet access, with 4G and 5G speeds up to a 20-mile radius, but it's most effective in about an eight-mile radius.

I located a radio tower in Jacksonville with space for rent. Then, I did something I had never done before. I climbed a tower to install my first WISP system. The testing I did after the installation was successful and I was able to provide customers within the radius of the antenna with high-speed internet.

Soon, I began to bring new customers onboard. I could definitely see the need and the value. That was made especially clear when schools were closed during the COVID-19 outbreak. Since classes moved online, many families were left behind because their children were in areas without internet access or with very limited or slow service.

The news aired a story about a boy in the fifth grade that they had learned was walking to his school every day, even though it was closed, just to be able to access the school's wi-fi system since he did not have internet service at home. The more I heard stories like that one, the more I knew I was venturing into a new business that did not just have enormous potential, but was also serving a great need. I felt really good knowing my new customers had children in the house who seriously needed my service.

Around the time the finishing touches were being made on this book, my YouTube marketing consulting work, my own YouTube channel and a new online radio station I was creating, were all taking up more and more of my time.

When I added my new community WISP service to my company, I knew I was at another crossroads in my life. Soon after that revelation, my wife and I made a road trip to sell most of my HVAC service equipment to another entrepreneur in the business.

Looking back on my life, I feel incredibly fortunate and grateful. I had found work I loved right out of high school. I found a great partner to share my life with in Kim, and we both, as well as our children, survived my serious injury and my time being held for a crime I did not commit.

The title of my book is true. I went from being wrongfully accused to success. That is one of the many reasons I feel blessed and thank God everyday for the life I have today. If you are battling serious issues in your own life, I sincerely hope you see my story as proof that, no matter what, there is always hope. I know many people who have suffered through a great deal more than I have. I think often of the others who have been incarcerated for a crime they didn't commit, too. I know many have likely died in prison never having their truth known. I also think of the many people who suffer other significant losses in their family, including sickness and death. When I look at life from that perspective, I see myself as one of the lucky ones.

Mike Powlas is the owner of Powlas Enterprises, a provider of rural broadband internet service through WISP systems.

He is also a consultant on using YouTube and other services to promote and expand small businesses.

www.ingramcontent.com/pod-product-compliance
Lightning Source LLC
Chambersburg PA
CBHW032042290426
44110CB00012B/920